GLOBAL ISSUES BIBLE STUDIES

Series editors: Stephen Hayner & Gordon Aeschliman

VOICELESS PEOPLE

Chuck Shelton

6 Studies
for individuals
or groups

INTERVARSITY PRESS
DOWNERS GROVE, ILLINOIS 60515

Please reply to:
Jonathan Lamb
16 Eden Drive
Oxford, OX3 0AB
Tel: 01865 760131

InterVarsity Press is the book-publishing division of InterVarsity Christian Fellowship, a student movement active on campus at hundreds of universities, colleges and schools of nursing in the United States of America, and a member movement of the International Fellowship of Evangelical Students. For information about local and regional activities, write Public Relations Dept., InterVarsity Christian Fellowship, 6400 Schroeder Rd., P.O. Box 7895, Madison, WI 53707-7895.

All Scripture quotations, unless otherwise indicated, are from the Holy Bible, New International Version. Copyright © 1973, 1978, International Bible Society. Used by permission of Zondervan Bible Publishers.

Cover illustration: TransLight

ISBN 0-8308-4912-2

Printed in the United States of America

12	11	10	9	8	7	6	5	4	3	2	1
99	98	97	96	95	94	93	92	91	90		

Contents

Because humankind is made in the image of God, every person, regardless of race, religion, color, culture, class, sex or age, has an intrinsic dignity because of which he or she should be respected and served, not exploited. Here too we express penitence both for our neglect and for having sometimes regarded evangelism and social concern as mutually exclusive.

Although reconciliation with people is not reconciliation with God, nor is social action evangelism, nor is political liberation salvation, nevertheless we affirm that evangelism and sociopolitical involvement are both part of our Christian duty. For both are necessary expressions of our doctrines of God and humankind, our love for our neighbor and our obedience to Jesus Christ.

The message of salvation implies also a message of judgment upon every form of alienation, oppression and discrimination, and we should not be afraid to denounce evil and injustice wherever they exist.

—*Lausanne Covenant, Article Five.*

Welcome to Global Issues Bible Studies

With all the rapid and dramatic changes happening in our world today, it's easy to be overwhelmed and simply withdraw. But it need not be so for Christians! God has not only given us the mandate to love the world, he has given us the Holy Spirit and the community of fellowship to guide us and equip us in the ministry of love.

Ministering in the world can be threatening: It requires change in both our lifestyle and our thinking. We end up discovering that we need to cling closer to Jesus than ever before—and that becomes the great personal benefit of change. God's love for the world is the same deep love he has for you and me.

This study series is designed to help us understand what is going on in *the world*. Then it takes us to *the Word* to help us be faithful in our compassionate response. The series is firmly rooted in the evangelical tradition which calls for a personal saving relationship with Jesus Christ and a public lifestyle of discipleship that demonstrates the Word has truly come alive in us.

At the front of the guide is an excerpt from the Lausanne Covenant which we have found particularly helpful. We have developed this series in keeping with the spirit of the covenant, especially sections four and five. You may wish to refer to the Lausanne Covenant for further guidance as you form your own theology of evangelism and social concern.

In the words of the covenant's authors we place this challenge before you: "The salvation we claim should be transforming us in the totality of our personal and social responsibilities. Faith without works is dead."

Getting the Most from Global Issues Bible Studies

Global Issues Bible Studies are designed to be an exciting and challenging way to help us seek God's will for all of the world as it is found in Scripture. As we learn more about the world, we will learn more about ourselves as well.

How They Are Designed

Global Issues Bible Studies have a number of distinctive features. First, each guide has an introduction from the author which will help orient us to the subject at hand and the significant questions which the studies will deal with.

Second, the Bible study portion is inductive rather than deductive. In other words, the author will lead us to discover what the Bible says about a particular topic through a series of questions rather than simply telling us what he or she believes. Therefore, the studies are thought-provoking. They help us to think about the meaning of the passage so that we can truly understand what the biblical writer intended to say.

Third, the studies are personal. Global Issues Bible Studies are not just theoretical studies to be considered in private or discussed in a group. These studies will motivate us to action. They will expose us to the promises, assurances, exhortations and challenges of God's

Word. Through the study of Scripture, we will renew our minds so that we can be transformed by the Spirit of God.

Fourth, the guides include resource sections that will help you to act on the challenges Scripture has presented you with.

Fifth, these studies are versatile. They are designed for student, mission, neighborhood and/or church groups. They are also effective for individual study.

How They Are Put Together

Global Issues Bible Studies also have a distinctive format. Each study need take no more than forty-five minutes in a group setting or thirty minutes in personal study—unless you choose to take more time.

Each guide has six studies. If the guides are used in pairs, they can be used within a quarter system in a church and fit well in a semester or trimester system on a college campus.

The guides have a workbook format with space for writing responses to each question. This is ideal for personal study and allows group members to prepare in advance for the discussion. In addition the last question in each study offers suggestions and opportunity for personal response.

At the end of the guides are some notes for leaders. They describe how to lead a group discussion, give helpful tips on group dynamics and suggest ways to deal with problems which may arise during the discussion. With such helps, someone with little or no experience can lead an effective study.

Suggestions for Individual Study

1. As you begin the study, pray that God will help you understand and apply the passages to your life. Pray that he will show you what kinds of action he would have you take as a result of your time of study.

2. In your first session take time to read the introduction to the entire guide. This will orient you to the subject at hand and the author's goals for the studies.

3. Read the short introduction to the study.

4. Read and reread the suggested Bible passages to familiarize yourself with them.

5. A good modern translation of the Bible, rather than the King James Version or a paraphrase, will give you the most help. The New International Version, the New American Standard Bible and the Revised Standard Version are all recommended. The questions in this guide are based on the New International Version.

6. Use the space provided to respond to the questions. This will help you express your understanding of the passage clearly.

7. Look up the passages listed under *For Further Study* at the end of each study. This will help you to better understand the principles outlined in the main passages and give you an idea of how these themes are found throughout Scripture.

8. It might be good to have a Bible dictionary handy. Use it to look up any unfamiliar words, names or places.

9. Take time with the final question in each study to commit yourself to action and/or a change in attitude.

Suggestions for Group Study

1. Come to the study prepared. Follow the suggestions for individual study mentioned above. You will find that careful preparation will greatly enrich your time spent in group discussion.

2. Be willing to participate in the discussion. The leader of your group will not be lecturing. Instead, he or she will be encouraging the members of the group to discuss what they have learned. The leader will be asking the questions that are found in this guide.

3. Stick to the topic being discussed. Your answers should be based on the verses which are the focus of the discussion and not on outside authorities such as commentaries or speakers.

4. Be sensitive to the other members of the group. Listen attentively when they describe what they have learned. You may be surprised by their insights! When possible, link what you say to the comments of others. Also, be affirming whenever you can. This will encourage

some of the more hesitant members of the group to participate.

5. Be careful not to dominate the discussion. We are sometimes so eager to express our thoughts that we leave too little opportunity for others to respond. By all means participate! But allow others to also.

6. Expect God to teach you through the passage being discussed and through the other members of the group. Pray that you will have an enjoyable and profitable time together, but also that as a result of the study, you will find ways that you can take action individually and/or as a group.

7. If you are the discussion leader, you will find additional suggestions at the back of the guide.

God bless you in your adventure of love.

Steve Hayner
Gordon Aeschliman

Introducing Voiceless People

Last summer I had the chance to visit the city of Manila—the capital of the Philippines. The teeming humidity and rain were a new experience for me, but my air-conditioned hotel provided comfort. The tropics are beautiful in their own way, and God has created in the people of the Philippines some of the warmest, most energetic and most hospitable folks in the world.

Along with brothers and sisters from around the world, I was surrounded by the glitter of an international Christian conference. It would have been possible to spend my ten days there absorbed in the ceremony, workshops and new relationships that were part of the conference. Or I could have played the tourist, merely sampling the exotic food and the bright sights of the city.

But God wouldn't leave me alone. On the way from the airport to the hotel I saw people who lived in huts of cardboard and aluminum sheets. I learned that the nightly price of my room at the Holiday Inn equaled a month's labor for the average hard-working Filipino.

From my room I viewed huge, expensive government buildings (including the convention site) constructed by the late dictator Ferdinand Marcos. In their shadows I saw a squalid, sprawling settlement of 15,000 homeless (unless you call tacked-together hovels of metal, bricks and bamboo a home).

Dirty, wet kids begged in broken English for money as I walked from the hotel to the opulent conference center. Traffic snarled every day, drivers honking in frustration from their smoke-belching vehicles.

I went jogging . . . once. Somehow it didn't refresh me to take a run past families living on the street, heavily armed police, and street sweepers who looked at me with blank (or were they surly?) eyes.

One day a group of us toured the city. The huge mall was packed with the Filipino middle-class. In the cathedral children begged us for money, as the priest read the story of the good Samaritan. At stop signs blind women led by their children implored us for a handout. But of all the people I saw, one in particular haunts me.

She was sitting in a deep puddle in the fast lane on a busy city street. (Actually, she must have been placed there, because she had lost both of her legs below the knee.) Rain torrents fell as the red light stopped us in the lane next to her. She looked directly at me with her quiet, liquid eyes and reached toward me with a plastic Coke cup in her hand. She was asking me to respond.

I was stunned by her presence and her need. I could not imagine what it was like to be that woman. One of the Filipino men in the van explained that she probably had been placed in the street to collect money for men who seek to profit through begging. To see her condition wounded my spirit, and to suspect she was being used in her powerlessness angered me.

As I rode on in the warm, dry van, the words of my Master echoed in my mind:

Then he will say to those on his left, "Depart from me, you who are cursed, into the eternal fire prepared for the devil and his angels. For I was hungry and you gave me nothing to eat, I was thirsty and you gave me nothing to drink, I was a stranger and you did not invite me in, I needed clothes and you did not clothe me, I was sick and in prison and you did not look after me."

They also will answer, "Lord, when did we see you hungry or thirsty or a stranger or needing clothes or sick or in prison, and did not help you?"

He will reply, "I tell you the truth, whatever you did not do for one of the least of these, you did not do for me."

Then they will go away to eternal punishment, but the righteous to eternal life. (Mt 25:41-46)

The woman I saw in Manila is "one of the least of these," a voiceless person. Through her, God spoke harshly in my ear.

Many of the voiceless are much closer to us than Manila. They are the handicapped, the urban and rural poor, abused women and children, the frail elderly, the unborn, the homeless, the hungry, the illiterate, the unemployed and people of color.

What does it mean to be voiceless? And what does God expect of Christians who have a voice? The purpose of these Bible studies is to examine these two questions.

The Disabilities of Power

People without voices are powerless and cannot speak for themselves. Their needs go unmet and they suffer. No one wants to hear the story of their lives.

In contrast, people with voices have power. If you graduate from a college or university, you are among the educated elite: one per cent of the world's population has a college degree. You may not feel all that powerful. If you're young, or still a student, you face limitations of many kinds. But let's take a look at your likely future:

☐ You will earn more money in one year than many Christians outside North America will earn in a lifetime.

☐ Your right to select your leaders through voting is secure.

☐ You will be able to purchase a home eventually and to consume a wide variety of products and services.

☐ Food will be plentiful.

☐ You will have access to the best health care in the world.

☐ Your children will be educated, and your parents will have the chance to age with dignity.

In short, you will be able to build for yourself and your family a life of comfort and opportunity.

As a Christian with a college education, you need to deal with the fact that you have power now and that your voice will be even more powerful later in life. The goal of coping with power isn't to position you to lord it over others (see Mt 20:25-28). You need to accept whatever power you've been granted and learn to submit your entire being to the Spirit of Christ living in you.

Power is the ability to control your own choices and the choices open to others. Such control is a precious commodity. But power is also a dangerous asset that can disable us in at least five ways:

1. The temptation to hubris. Hubris is a Greek word for insufferable pride in human effort. The ability to control our own choices and the choices of others (power) fuels itself through the self-centered presumption that we are the source of our own power. "The earth is the LORD's, and everything in it" (Ps 24:1). "There is no authority except that which God has established" (Rom 13:1). Therefore, any power we possess is derived from our Creator. We are wholly accountable to God for the way we exercise it.

2. The arrogance of advantage. One of the great temptations of power is to do things to people. History abounds with examples, and Christians, being fully human, often participate in victimization.

One of the great lies of power is that its possession entitles us to do things for people. In relating to the less fortunate we think we have much to give but nothing to get. We say, "Let's help these poor folks out."

I'm not criticizing free turkeys at Thanksgiving. But the prosperous have created a welfare-mentality because we use our advantage arrogantly to do things for people. Christians exercising power must be totally committed to working with and among the voiceless. The powerless have a great deal to teach us. God spoke directly to me through the Filipina in the puddle.

3. Deafness to vulnerability. To be precise, it's not that powerless people don't have voices. The truth is that we the powerful are mostly deaf to their need. Their voices ring in God's ears, while the Lord's hands here on earth (that is, believers) are slow to respond.

It's easy to get entirely caught up in the daily activities of a comfortable life: education, romance, family and friends, profession, church, recreation, shopping, travel. The homeless become a nuisance. Urban poverty is an impolite reality we become skilled at overlooking. The fact that people are dying of hunger as we read this might motivate us just enough to fling up a brief prayer for them and to write a quick relief check. While our taxes pay for American foreign policies that encourage poverty and war, we consider such issues only during national elections—if then.

If we don't allow ourselves to hear the voiceless, we will be disabled by hardness of heart.

4. Living as nerds and wimps. Sometimes our response to the voiceless is one of ineffectiveness and impotence. We run the risk of living as prosperous Christian nerds and wimps.

A nerd doesn't know how to act in a manner appropriate to the situation. Similarly, when we isolate ourselves from someone in pain, we respond inappropriately to a person in need. When we wrap ourselves in our own social circles, we mock the very Jesus whose name we claim as Christians.

Wimps, on the other hand, don't respond at all because they're . . . well, wimps! They are weak-kneed and unable to do what needs to be done. The objective reality is, of course, that people's needs outstrip our ability to help. I can't personally help all the babies born in my city suffering from AIDS or cocaine addiction. None of our families can help all the sexually abused women and children in our town. No single congregation will be able to provide the community development services a poor neighborhood needs.

But God is thoroughly unimpressed with our limitations. Throughout the Old Testament God harshly judges those who do not respond appropriately to the needs of the poor. And Jesus will render the same judgment (see Mt 25:41-46). It is pathetic when Christians with abundant resources spend much of their money and time in pursuit of their own comfort. We don't know how to learn from and serve the voiceless because we don't try!

Our skyscrapers shine and our churches prosper. Yet for all the trappings of power, the wealthy of the world (and we must count ourselves among them) usually aren't willing to invest what we have to provide for basic human needs. We shouldn't be surprised that a secular society is so selfish. But it is shocking that so many Christians are wimps in the face of human need, impotent to respond in any meaningful way.

5. The lack of a world Christian perspective. Finally, we can be disabled by the power we possess through a stunted view of our status in the world. From my suburban home I moved from high school through college to graduate school, pursuing opportunities as they came to me. It was only after graduate school that I learned this fact: a young black man in California is more likely to be murdered than he is to have the academic qualifications to apply to a University of California school.

I would have pursued my education the same way even if I'd known this fact earlier. But I would have viewed myself and my options with a more informed perspective. I would hope that that knowledge would have shaped the way I related to and prayed for African-American men my age.

Those of us from middle- and upper-middle-class homes tend to view the world from the perspective of a half-full or empty glass—sometimes we sense that we have more advantages than many people do, and at other times we can only see what we don't have.

We must learn to look at our lives through the eyes of a voiceless person. An illiterate Hispanic brother in Christ would view your struggle to select a major or a graduate school differently from the way you do: he would be thrilled with the chance just to get an education. A poor Christian sister on a Mohawk reservation might see your hassles with your roommate in another light: she would just like to have running water and electricity for her family. Your apartment would do nicely.

Some educators say that college students aren't likely to embrace a world perspective because they are so caught up in the developmental dynamics of young adulthood. But I don't believe the Holy Spirit waits until some magic moment in our mid-twenties to start fostering in each Christian a conscience and a compassionate world view.

To mature in the Lord you must develop and frequently call to mind a perspective of your life informed by what the voiceless see when they look at you. The powerless live an almost-empty-glass life, while the objective reality of your life (by comparison) resembles a half-full tanker truck.

Let me be explicit: We shouldn't scorn our opportunities, choose powerlessness or become obsessed with guilt over comforts we do enjoy. God created a world in which people are meant to experience love and find adequate food, shelter, safety, health and meaningful work. Granting its many shortcomings, North America is a land that provides to millions the chance for such a life. We should praise Jesus for the freedom and opportunity we do experience. This prosperity means, however, that we must energetically deal with the way that power can disable us.

The suffering of the disadvantaged should cause us to look to the wellspring of active compassion in our own hearts. With fear and trembling we must cope with our advantages, or the voiceless will never be heard and served. We will answer to God for their oppression. And we will have missed the opportunity to hear the voice of Jesus through them.

Life in the Spirit
What does God expect of Christians who have a voice? Whatever our status in human society, the Lord seeks the same from all people.

The challenges of discipleship differ depending on income, race, gender, nationality, education and how we were raised. And "from everyone who has been given much, much will be demanded" (Lk 12:48). To whatever degree we have the ability to control our own choices, all Christians are the same before God.

What are some of the particular discipleship challenges for Christians concerned about voiceless people? Let's look at three:

1. Friendship with God. We must never take lightly our personal relationship with Jesus Christ. Compassion for the less fortunate can flow only out of a deepening spiritual sense that God aches for voiceless people. And we will sustain our care for those in pain only when our hearts are continually broken by the things that break the heart of God.

We will often feel powerless as we open ourselves up to the alienation and hopelessness of the poor. We will learn to depend on the Holy Spirit to bring before the Lord our inmost concerns. It is not a coincidence that the letter of James discusses issues of preferring rich over poor and living an active faith (Jas 2) and then counsels, "Come near to God and he will come near to you" (Jas 4:8).

To experience the Lord's compassion personally will foster in us a reservoir of concern for others. Only careful attention to your friendship with Jesus will help you overcome the disabilities of pride, arrogance and hardness of heart.

2. The courage to listen. Ears are made for receiving aural messages to the brain. And our ears seem to work best when those messages are good news. It takes a special commitment to listen to people living through tough times. There are so many encouraging voices we prefer to hear: inspirational songs, the warm tones of our loved ones, the laughter of friends, a challenging lecture. In our feel-good society, why would any sane person seek out those in pain?

We'd rather get insight from the Lord via good-looking messengers, great sermons and first-rate Christian music. It is easier not to listen to the small voices of hurting people. If we listen too long, we might get in touch with our own pain. Wouldn't it be just like the

God of the Bible to speak to us through some struggling person or through our own hurt?

This is no 7-Eleven God we serve. The Master of our lives is not convenient. Born in a barn, he came to a poor family. He was rude to religious professionals, but he let prostitutes and bleeding women touch him; he comforted the mourning and calmed the fearful.

It takes a measure of confidence to listen to people with less power. But it isn't confidence in ourselves. Only confidence in the patience and the power of Jesus Christ will bring about in us a lifestyle of intentional, rather than casual, compassion.

3. The nerve to speak and act. Do you energetically pursue your friendship with God? Are you learning to listen for God's voice in the pained voices of those less fortunate than you?

You can't be an advocate for the poor until you learn from the poor. And even if you have a great deal of experience among voiceless people, you must be very careful. Christian advocacy is entirely accountable to those whose plight you are representing. And it is risky to speak such truth to the powers that be.

For instance, every university campus should do more to address racial conflict and reconciliation. But students of color will participate with you only if they trust you. And trust can grow only with time, proximity and kept promises. At the same time other Anglo students (some of them Christians) will consider you a left-leaning liberal socialist. A ministry of reconciliation is costly.

Let's be honest. Most Christians suffer from moral laryngitis. We don't like to speak about justice. We don't like to behave assertively by standing up for what's right or opposing what's wrong. It doesn't seem polite, and if evangelicals are anything, they are polite. Of course, only the privileged preach the gospel of maintaining the status quo. "Don't rock the lifeboat" is the survivors' chorus. Drowning people are just trying to catch their next breath.

This isn't a prescription for becoming a flaming radical. But if our hearts have been broken by the things that break the heart of God, we will have the humility to learn from the voiceless. And we will be given the nerve to speak and act appropriately in response to their needs. Jesus will speak to you through the voiceless and change you into the image of Christ. It won't be easy, but it will be good.

Study 1

Who We Are

Only when we understand our identity as created beings will we live as our Creator intends. Any resources we possess are from God's hand—unless they are ill-gotten (family wealth built upon the labor of the poor, for example).

Voiceless people do not have the same advantages that we do and are, therefore, not able to control their own choices. Those who are powerless need our friendship. And if we are willing to learn from the less fortunate, God will speak to us through them.

The prosperous and the voiceless need each other because of our common identity before God. All the power in this world exists at our Creator's discretion. We must understand who we are in God if we intend to utilize the resources we have for the sake of the voiceless.

1. Think of a time when you felt voiceless. Describe both how you wanted to be treated by those who had power and how you were actually treated.

How did you feel in this situation?

Read Genesis 1:26-28 to review the story of the origins of human-kind.
2. What are the various meanings of the word *image*?

3. What does it mean to you personally to be created in the image of God?

4. What reasons do you think God had for creating humans male and female?

5. How does gender relate to issues of power?

Read Matthew 25:31-46 in which Jesus tells us one way to recognize his presence in our lives.

6. Mother Teresa said of her life in the streets of Calcutta: "We try to pray through our work by doing it with Jesus, for Jesus, to Jesus. That helps us put our whole heart and soul into doing it. The dying, the crippled, the mentally ill, the unwanted, the unloved—they are Jesus in disguise." Why does Jesus disguise himself in such people?

7. Who are the people in need, and how are we to respond to them (vv. 35-36)?

8. Note how Jesus in Matthew links recognition of the disadvantaged with a response to their needs. What is the link between belief and behavior in your life?

9. Describe a personal encounter you have had with one whom Jesus describes as "the least of these" (v. 45).

10. Sometimes we pass by "the least of these" without offering help. What are some of the reasons that we choose to overlook voiceless people?

How do our actions differ from Jesus' response?

11. *Response:* Take time this week to thank God for the gift of Jesus. Ask him to fill you with his Holy Spirit, revealing to you the image of God in voiceless people so that you might serve and learn from these brothers and sisters in Christ.

For Further Study: Ephesians 2:10.

Study 2

Our Need
for God

We will benefit in at least three ways if we nurture an intimate sense of our need for God as we relate to voiceless people. First, we will develop the discipline of facing pain in the lives of others and in our own lives. This isn't "holy masochism"—certainly there is no virtue in suffering itself. But there are too many temptations to unending comfort. Our pleasure must not be our primary concern when thousands of our brothers and sisters starve to death each day.

Second, to understand and respond to the voiceless, we must have the gumption to face their needs. This takes courage, as these needs are profound, and our resources are limited. Prayer and fasting are key tools for building such fortitude.

Do you earnestly deal with sin in your life? While the ultimate effect of sin (separation from God) is death, one of the immediate effects of our sin is to deny people the chance to live with the dignity God intends. Repentance, the third quality, emerges from our daily experience of the need for God. To repent in relation to voiceless people means "to turn away from behavior which directly or indirectly oppresses the disadvantaged."

1. At various times in our lives, we have sinned against others. Our sin may include a specific failure to respond to persons who were in pain, or an indirect sin through involvement in an oppressive system or organization. Trusting in God's mercy, identify two things you have done that may have caused a voiceless person to suffer.

Read Isaiah 59 for a description of our world and our participation in it.
2. According to this passage, God is able to hear our voice, but our sin prevents him. Identify ten of the sins that separate us from God (vv. 3-8).

3. Describe a current situation in your country that reflects Isaiah 59:7-8.

4. Verses 9-11 make vivid the daily experience of powerless people. Describe a time in your life when you felt this way.

5. What is the implication of sin in our lives (vv. 12-13)?

6. What effects do our sins against those who are powerless have on the world (vv. 13-15)?

7. How is God's reaction described in verses 15-16?

8. God answers our transgressions with righteousness, salvation, vengeance and zeal (v. 17). Why are those four responses appropriate?

9. What does it mean to "fear" God (v. 19)?

10. What does God promise to those "who repent of their sins" (vv. 20-21)?

11. *Response:* Take time each day this week to confess to the Lord your need for him. Ask him to help you recognize and turn away from any act, attitude or passivity that separates you from God and other people.

For Further Study: Romans 3:8-18; Psalm 25; Philippians 2:12-13.

God's Answer to Our Needs

Although *we're created in the likeness of God, we've separated* ourselves from our Creator. We may not mistreat voiceless people directly. But we prosper through an economic and political system that victimizes some and neglects many.

It is likely that we know very few people who might be called voiceless. We carefully avoid associating with them. We certainly don't go looking for someone in pain when we want to hear from Jesus.

In fact, the whole idea of God speaking to us through the oppressed seems like a perverse joke. Our God is the God of joy, and we want to be happy. Western Christians seek physical and mental health, a nice home and two cars, well-mannered children, long vacations, and a conflict-free church.

None of these aspirations is innately evil. Our Creator intended from the beginning that humankind should experience fulfilling and comfortable lives. God desires for each of us a life in which love and a vocation of service are everyday realities. The Lord wants to reign through justice in our societies and through peace between adversaries.

What do we need, then? If we define our needs in terms of possessions, then we don't need God; a vibrant capitalism with some heart will be adequate. But if our true need is for a healed relationship with God, we must seek a relationship with him that remolds us into the image in which we were created.

God's answer to our need is found in the person of Jesus. We need to be transformed into the image of Christ, the one who reconciled us to God through the cross. This sounds great, and it is! But there is no discipleship without relationship. And any authentic relationship is costly, uncomfortable and full of interruptions.

1. When are you most aware of God's presence with you?

Read Luke 4:16-21 for God's response to our need to be in a relationship with him.
2. How does Jesus know the Spirit of God is with him (v. 18)?

3. Identify the people/situations described in verse 18 as you see

them in the world today. (Who are the poor, imprisoned, blind and/
or oppressed people?)

Read Isaiah 61.
4. List ten actions to be taken by a person on whom the Spirit of
the Lord rests (vv. 1-4).

Beside each of these actions list an example of what living it out
would look like on your campus, in your family, church or community. (For example, working on a Habitat for Humanity project to
build housing with the poor would "repair the ruined city.")

5. Isaiah 61:5-11 (and much of the rest of the Bible) calls us toward
an ultimate reality that will come to pass only partially this side of
heaven. How much of God's ultimate will for earth can we participate in here and now?

6. What does it mean to be clothed with "garments of salvation" and "arrayed in a robe of righteousness" (v. 10)?

7. How does verse 11 provide encouragement as you seek to be a voice for the voiceless?

8. *Response:* Examine your life for opportunities to offer help and encouragement to the poor, imprisoned, blind and oppressed people that you are aware of. Plan into your schedule exactly when and how you will take these actions.

For Further Study: Ephesians 2:1-10.

The People Jesus Sought

We've looked at how each person has been created to share the likeness of God. We've considered just how far we've diverged from a right relationship with our Creator and "the least of these"—the voiceless. And we've welcomed God's response to our sinful nature and lifestyle in the person of Jesus Christ.

With Jesus as our mentor, we need to examine our own involvement with the disadvantaged (or the lack of it). We will discover more about our own relationship to our Master as we explore how he related to voiceless people.

1. Jesus expects us to serve the poor as if each voiceless person were

Jesus himself. Describe what this service would look like.

Read the following passages describing Jesus' ministry in the Gospel of Luke: 5:8, 12-13, 18-20; 6:6-10, 17-19; 7:10, 11-15.
2. List the troubles of the people Jesus serves in these passages.

3. If these people were all in the same room, what sort of a group would it be before they met Jesus?

What would they be like after encountering him?

4. Such a group, after being healed by Jesus, gives us a picture of the church. What happens to us when we forget how sick we were prior to the intervention of God?

5. Compile your own list of such broken people in the modern world. How do you think Jesus would seek to bind the wounded if he came now? Would he intervene in their lives personally or pursue his mission through another avenue, such as church leadership, education, business, the media, politics or community development?

6. In Luke 6:6-11 the Pharisees complained about Jesus' healing ministry. What is their complaint?

7. What do you think might have been the deeper reasons for their fury as it is described in verse 11?

Read Luke 5:30-32.

8. Religious professionals were criticizing Jesus for associating with unclean people. Describe similar reactions you have seen from Christian leaders who are uncomfortable with the voiceless today.

How would Jesus respond to them (vv. 31-32)?

9. Jesus says he came to heal the sick, not the healthy. What does that mean for you as someone potentially headed for prosperity and power?

10. *Response:* Go on a fast for a day, drinking only water. Focus your prayers on the Holy Spirit, asking to be empowered to learn from and care for voiceless people near you.

For Further Study: Luke 4:18-19, 40-41; 7:22, 37-48.

Hearing and Doing the Will of God

In high school I was taught that all you have to do to be a Christian is to confess your sin and ask Jesus into your life. I've discovered since then that it's a lie.

At least it's a lie if we stop there. Certainly confession and invitation are acts of the will as we enter into new life in Christ. But we're not born again to live as infants. A spiritual birth without discipleship is a stillbirth.

The primary Christian activity of many is to come together to talk and sing about Jesus. But talk is cheap and easy. Discipleship is costly and difficult. We must choose: either we are absolutely and radically submitted to the reign of Jesus in our lives, or we're just consumers shopping the religion market.

If you boil down life in Christ to the essentials, you've got five daily disciplines:

1. Examine your attitudes and actions for evidence of sin, and

return to your best understanding of God's will for your life.

2. Seek the presence of the Holy Spirit in your life.

3. Rejoice in the love and unmerited favor God showers upon you. Wrestle with God over what you don't understand about his will in your life.

4. Participate in fellowship with believers who pursue these same disciplines.

5. Discover what God is doing in the world and join in. Live openly and authentically as a Christian among family, friends, coworkers and adversaries.

A passive attitude toward maturing in the faith is extremely dangerous for a Christian. Don't risk it.

1. What is your understanding of the relationship between faith and works?[1]

Read Luke 6:46-49.

2. According to this passage, how are we to hear Jesus' voice (v. 47)?

3. At what times in your life can you recall being most and/or least able to hear the voice of Jesus? Why?

4. How are you building the "foundation" that Jesus speaks of in verse 48?

Read Romans 2:1-13.

5. How do we (as individuals and as a culture) "pass judgment" (v. 1) on the poor and the oppressed?

6. How do we show "contempt for the riches of his kindness, tolerance and patience" (v. 4) in the ways we relate (or don't relate) to voiceless people?

7. What does Romans 2:6 mean for you in your vocation?

8. What is at stake in verses 6-10?

How do you react to these verses?

Read Matthew 11:25-30.
9. How do these verses give you comfort and joy in light of the great calling in Romans 2?

10. *Response:* The ultimate result of disobedience and hardness of heart described in Romans 2 is serious. Pray fervently that the Lord will break your heart with the things that break his heart.

For Further Study: Matthew 7:21-23.

---

[1]If you are unsure of what you think about the relationship between faith and works, you may wish to do further study in this area. Begin with Romans 2:6-13 and 3:20-26, Ephesians 2:1-10 and James 1:19—2:26.

Responsibility

We've examined what it means to be created in the image of God and how we share that image with the voiceless. We've recognized our profound need for God's compassion. And we explored how relationship is the Lord's answer to our need. Jesus speaks to us directly, but he also allows us to hear his voice indirectly—through the voiceless. Finally, we have struggled with the challenge of hearing and doing the will of God.

Responsibility is a one-word summary of life in Christ. Because we hear God's voice, we obey. Out of experiencing the Lord's forgiveness and compassion, we respond to others with whom we share the Creator's image with grace and care. We close this series on voiceless people by considering what it takes to worship and serve Jesus Christ.

1. Think of a time when you felt incapable of responding to a human need. What would have enabled you to respond?

Read 1 John 3:11-18.
2. How does John contrast love and hate in verses 11-16?

3. Who is "the world" in verse 13?

4. Why does the world hate us for seeking to live through love and sacrifice?

5. As a Christian, have you ever experienced the hate of the world? Describe the situation.

6. Verses 15 and 16 are opposites. What are the implications of these

verses for the way we relate to the disadvantaged? (Consider, for example, your attitude toward people of other races or those in poverty.)

7. Don't shy away from facing the enormous pain in the world, but don't let it paralyze you. The most important thing is to take one small step at a time to serve and learn from one voiceless person. How do you live out verse 17 by giving your resources to your brother in need?[1]

8. The early Christian leader Augustine wrote: "Pray as though everything depends on God. Work as though everything depends on you." How could this saying shape your ability to respond to voiceless people?

9. *Response:* Return to Isaiah 61. In study three, question four, we listed ten actions which could be taken on the part of voiceless people. Select one and start acting on it this week.

Prayer: The desire of every human heart—whether we live in prosperity or as people whose voices go unheard—is to know the Lord. Let us pray together: "Guide us continually, Lord; satisfy us with good things and bring us health. Tend our lives as a watered garden, and flow through us like a never-failing spring of water, where the parched may be refreshed. In our Lord Jesus Christ, Amen."

For Further Study: Isaiah 58.

---

[1]*Some suggestions:* Find out about a few local programs for the homeless, support them financially as you're able, and encourage street people who ask you for help to benefit from these programs. Carry a couple of apples to give away when you're in the city. Pray and work for social solutions to the plight of homeless people. Volunteer for a program serving the homeless, and encourage your friends to help as well.

Suggestions for Leaders

Leading a Bible discussion can be an enjoyable and rewarding experience. But it can also be intimidating—especially if you've never done it before. If this is how you feel, you're in good company. When God asked Moses to lead the Israelites out of Egypt, he replied, "O Lord, please send someone else to do it!" (Ex 4:13). But God's response to all of his servants—including you—is essentially the same: "My grace is sufficient for you" (2 Cor 12:9).

There is another reason you should feel encouraged. Leading a Bible discussion is not difficult if you follow certain guidelines. You don't need to be an expert on the Bible or a trained teacher. The suggestions listed below should enable you to effectively and enjoyably fulfill your role as leader.

Preparing for the Study

1. Ask God to help you understand and apply the passage in your own life. Unless this happens, you will not be prepared to lead others. Pray too for the various members of the group. Ask God to open your hearts to the message of his Word and motivate you to action.

2. Read the introduction to the entire guide to get an overview of the subject at hand and the issues which will be explored. If you want to do more reading on the topic, check out the resource section at the end of the guide for appropriate books and magazines.

3. As you begin each study, read and reread the assigned Bible passages to familiarize yourself with them. Read the passages suggested for further study as well. This will give you a broader picture of how these issues are discussed throughout Scripture.

4. This study guide is based on the New International Version of the Bible. It will help you and the group if you use this translation as the basis for your study and discussion.

5. Carefully work through each question in the study. Spend time in meditation and reflection as you consider how to respond.

6. Write your thoughts and responses in the space provided in the study guide. This will help you to express your understanding of the passage clearly.

7. It might help you to have a Bible dictionary handy. Use it to look up any unfamiliar words, names or places. (For additional help on how to study a passage, see chapter five of *Leading Bible Discussions,* IVP.)

8. Take the response portion of each study seriously. Consider what this means for your life—what changes you might need to make in your lifestyle and/or actions you need to take in the world. Remember that the group will follow your lead in responding to the studies.

Leading the Study

1. Begin the study on time. Open with prayer, asking God to help the group to understand and apply the passage.

2. Be sure that everyone in your group has a study guide. Encourage the group to prepare beforehand for each discussion by reading the introduction to the guide and by working through the questions in the study.

3. At the beginning of your first time together, explain that these studies are meant to be discussions, not lectures. Encourage the members of the group to participate. However, do not put pressure on those who may be hesitant to speak during the first few sessions.

4. Have a group member read the introductory paragraph at the beginning of the discussion. This will orient the group to the topic of the study.

5. Have a group member read aloud the passage to be studied. (When there is more than one passage, the Scripture is divided up throughout the study so that you won't have to keep several passages in mind at the same time.)

6. As you ask the questions, keep in mind that they are designed to be used just as they are written. You may simply read them aloud. Or you may prefer to express them in your own words. There may be times when it is appropriate to deviate from the study guide. For example, a question may have already been answered. If so, move on to the next question. Or someone may raise an important question not covered in the guide. Take time to discuss it, but try to keep the group from going off on tangents.

7. Avoid answering your own questions. If necessary, repeat or rephrase them until they are clearly understood. An eager group quickly becomes passive and silent if they think the leader will do most of the talking.

8. Don't be afraid of silence. People may need time to think about the question before formulating their answers.

9. Don't be content with just one answer. Ask, "What do the rest of you think?" or "anything else?" until several people have given answers to the question.

10. Acknowledge all contributions. Try to be affirming whenever possible. Never reject an answer. If it is clearly off-base, ask, "Which verse led you to that conclusion?" or again, "What do the rest of you think?"

11. Don't expect every answer to be addressed to you, even though this will probably happen at first. As group members become more at ease, they will begin to truly interact with each other. This is one sign of healthy discussion.

12. Don't be afraid of controversy. It can be very stimulating. If you don't resolve an issue completely, don't be frustrated. Move on and keep it in mind for later. A subsequent study may solve the problem.

13. Periodically summarize what the group has said about the passage. This helps to draw together the various ideas mentioned and gives continuity to the study. But don't preach.

14. Don't skip over the response question. Be willing to get things started by describing how you have been convicted by the study and what action you'd like to take. Consider doing a service project as a group in response to what you're learning from the studies. Alternately, hold one another accountable to get involved in some kind of active service.

15. Conclude your time together with conversational prayer. Ask for God's help in following through on the commitments you've made.

16. End on time.

Many more suggestions and helps are found in *The Small Group Leader's Handbook* and *Good Things Come in Small Groups* (both from IVP). Reading through one of these books would be worth your time.

Resources

Contact InterVarsity's headquarters in Madison, Wisconsin, at (608) 274-9001 and ask for the Multi-Ethnic Ministries Department. Find out if they are active in your area and whom you can contact to get involved.

Contact a respected ministry that works with disadvantaged people in your area. Visit and/or volunteer some of your time, to have the opportunity to learn from the voiceless.

Organizations

Bread for the World, 802 Rhode Island Ave. N.E., Washington, D.C. 20018. An advocacy organization for Christians concerned with hunger and food policy.

Evangelicals for Social Action, 10 Lancaster Ave., Philadelphia, Pa. 19151; (215) 645-9390. A Christian membership organization with local chapters, "promoting shalom in public life."

Habitat for Humanity, Habitat & Church Aves., Americus, Ga. 31709; (912) 924-6935. Builds and renovates housing with poor families and Christian volunteers. Church and student groups work on local projects.

MAP International, 2200 Glynco Parkway, Brunswick, Ga. 31520.

The Obsidian Society, 236 N. Madison Ave., Pasadena,, Calif. 91101; (818) 449-8116. A fellowship equipping Christians to lead in racially diverse settings in society and the church.

SIM International, 2 Woodstone Dr., Cedar Grove, N.J. 07009.

Transformation International, 1050 17th St. N.W., Suite 820, Washington, D.C. 20036.

World Concern, 19303 Fremont Ave. N., Seattle, Wash. 98133.

World Relief, P.O. Box WRC, Wheaton, Ill.; (708) 665-0235. An evangelical relief and development ministry, with direct involvement in refugee ministry in many areas of the United States.

World Vision, 919 W. Huntington Dr., Monrovia, Calif. 91016.

Publications

Cornerstone, 4707 North Malden, Chicago, Ill. 60640 (312) 989-2080. A monthly magazine published by Jesus People, USA.

Houston, James. *The Transforming Friendship: A Guide to Prayer.* Batavia, Ill.: Lion Publishing Corp., 1989. A thoughtful and practical look at prayer as friendship with God.

Sine, Tom. *Unleashing a Wild Hope.* Waco, Tex.: Word, 1990.

Sojourners, Box 29272, Washington, D.C. 20017. A monthly magazine and other educational resources on radical Christian discipleship.

World Christian, P.O. Box 40010, Pasadena, Calif. 91114; (818) 797-1907. A monthly magazine on world mission, evangelism and justice for committed Christians.

Wallis, Jim. *Call to Conversion: Recovering the Gospel for These Times.* New York: Harper & Row, 1983.